101 Amazing Things to Do in Sweden

© 2018 101 Amazing Things

All rights reserved. No part of this publication may be reproduced, distributed, or transmitted in any form or by any means, including photocopying, recording, or other electronic or mechanical methods, without the prior written permission of the publisher, except in the case of brief quotations embodied in critical reviews and certain other noncommercial uses permitted by copyright law.

Introduction

So you're going to Sweden, huh? You are very luck indeed! You are sure in for a treat because Sweden is, without a doubt, one of the most special travel destinations on the face of the earth – and so criminally underrated. It offers something for every visitor, so whether you are into exploring the local gastronomic scene, buying some special items of Scandi-design, or hiking in the deep forest, Sweden has something that you'll treasure.

This guide will take you on a journey from the major cities like Stockholm, Gothenburg, Uppsala, and Malmo, and into the countryside, Swedish Lapland, and the islands to boot.

In this guide, we'll be giving you the low down on:
- the very best things to shove in your pie hole, whether you need to want to chow down on traditional Swedish sausages, or you want to have a Michelin star fine dining experience
- incredible festivals, from electronic festivals with world famous headliners through to the Stockholm Early Music Festival

- the coolest historical and cultural sights that you simply cannot afford to miss like Swedish art fairs, and ancient castles and fortresses
- the most incredible outdoor adventures, whether you want to hike through Swedish Lapland or have at dog sledding
- where to shop for authentic souvenirs so that you can remember your trip to Sweden forever
- the places where you can party like a local and make new friends
- and tonnes more coolness besides!

Let's not waste any more time — here are the 101 most amazing, spectacular, and coolest things not to miss in Sweden!

1. Take a Guided Tour of Stadshuset, Stockholm's City Hall

Stockholm is a very beautiful city, and in no small part because of the stunning buildings that line the city streets. City Hal, known as Stadshuset locally, is equal parts beautiful and important. It is famed for its grand ceremonial halls, and wonderful works of art. It's also a functioning government building, with offices for 200 people inside. We think that one of the best ways to get to know this building is by taking one of the group tours.

(Hantverkargatan 1, 111 52 Stockholm; www.stockholm.se/OmStockholm/Stadshuset)

2. Sleep in a Treehouse at the Treehotel

If you like the idea of getting back to nature and sleeping in woods, but know yourself too well to expose yourself to nature's critters and creepy crawlies, we think that the Treehotel could be right up your alley. Yes, this is a hotel that specialises in its treehouse style rooms, but always with a boutique twist. There's also a tree sauna on-site so that you can relax, indulge, and let the weight of the world fall from your shoulders.

(Edeforsvägen 2A, 960 24 Harads; www.treehotel.se/en)

3. Enjoy Summer Cocktails on a Floating Pontoon

We think that Sweden is an awesome holiday destination at any time of year, but it does take a brave soul to visit in the winter time when it's very cold and dark. If you prefer the idea of lounging in the Swedish sunshine with a cocktail in your hand, be sure to visit Stockholm in the summer months, and pay a visit to Malarpaviljongen, a floating pontoon, while you're there. There's a seasonal menu, a gorgeous garden area, and a cocktail menu to die for.

(Norr Mälarstrand 64, 112 35 Stockholm; http://malarpaviljongen.se)

4. Check Out the Art Installations of the Stockholm Metro System

While it's true that Stockholm doesn't have as many museums and galleries as some other European cities, this really doesn't matter because there's an artistic experience everywhere you look. In fact, the city's metro system is the world's longest art exhibit, spanning 110 kilometres, with art installations throughout. 90 out of 100 of the stations are filled with paintings, mosaics, sculptures, engravings, reliefs, and more, and the city even puts on guided tours of all this underground beauty.

(www.visitstockholm.com/en/See--do/Attractions/art-in-the-subway)

5. Enjoy a Traditional Swedish Bun, Semla

The people of Sweden do love to sit down at any time of day with a strong cup of coffee and a pastry. But not just any pastry will do when you are in Sweden, and we highly recommend that you get your chops around a Semla, a Swedish type of bun that is decadent in all the best ways. These are traditionally eaten the day before Lent, but can actually be found all the time, and consist of a fluffy bun that is cut and half, and spread with almond-cardamom paste and light vanilla whipped cream.

6. Take in All the Glory of Uppsala Cathedral

When you think of gorgeous church architecture around Europe, it's likely that you'll first think about places like Italy and France, but believe us when we say that Sweden has its fair share of beautiful church architecture, and the most beautiful of them all is Uppsala Cathedral, which also happens to be the largest cathedral in the whole of Scandinavia. It dates way back to the 13th century, and is open to visitors every day.

(Domkyrkoplan, 753 10 Uppsala; www.svenskakyrkan.se/uppsala/domkyrkan)

7. Enjoy the Creepy Festivities of Walpurgisnacht

Walpurgisnacht, April 30th, is one of the most fun times to be in Sweden. This tradition actually originates from Germany, and is said to commemorate the meeting of a group of witches in wooded hills in Germany. This is all very fun, but in Sweden the emphasis is more on the arrival of springtime and the sunny weather. Traditionally, bonfires are lit, and people sing songs of welcome to Spring late into the night while warming themselves with bowls of nettle soup.

8. Explore all the Majesty of the Vasa Museum

Stockholm is a city made up of islands, right on the coast of Sweden, and this means that water and sailing play a huge part in the history and culture of this beautiful place.

There's no doubt that the best place to learn about this history is at the Vasa Museum. It displays the world's only fully intact 17th century ship that has been salvaged, and ten different exhibits around the ship that tell you about life on the ship and how it contributed to Stockholm's history.

(Galärvarvsvägen 14, 115 21 Stockholm; www.vasamuseet.se)

9. Enjoy Concerts With a Difference at the Stockholm Early Music Festival

For culture lovers, Stockholm is a city with endless rewards, and if it's music that really gets you going, we think you'd be wise to plan your trip to coincide with the annual Early Musical Festival, which takes place every June in the city. This festival is completely dedicated to Baroque, Renaissance, and Medieval music, with a diverse programme of music events with musicians from all over the world taking to the stage.

(www.semf.se)

10. Have a Dog Sledding Adventure in Swedish Lapland

We cannot lie; Sweden is cold and dark in the winter time. But if you are brave enough to tackle the below freezing temperatures, a magical wintry world awaits you, particularly if you can make it to the far north of the country in Swedish Lapland. There are many companies and tour groups in this part of the country that can offer dog sledding in the snow. This is a particularly magical experience for young children.

11. Control the Stockholm Light Tower With Your Smartphone

One of the most unique buildings that you will see in Stockholm will almost certainly be the Stockholm Light Tower, and in no small part because of the Colour by Numbers light installation that it has. Just by standing on the site, you have the ability to change the colours of the lights at the top of the building with nothing but your smartphone, and they'll be seen by everyone in the city. If that's not mega-cool, we just don't know what is.

(www.colourbynumbers.org/en/still.html)

12. Challenge Yourself With the Kungsleden Hiking Trail

If you want to totally immerse yourself in the stunning landscapes of northern Sweden and you aren't afraid to leave behind your creature comforts, we would love to let you know about the Kungsleden Hiking Trail, which is by no means an easy hike. This is one for experienced hikers since it covers 440 kilometres of land, and if you want to cover the whole thing, it will take you around four weeks. It's split up into four sections, so you can also cover shorter spans of the trail. It's only possible to hike the trail from June to September.

13. Visit the World's Oldest Tree, Old Tjikko

Sweden is certainly a place that offers endless exploration for nature lovers. Forests abound, and among the trees of the forest there is one tree that is very special indeed, because Old Tjikko is in fact the oldest known tree in the whole world. This 13 foot tall Christmas tree doesn't look all that spectacular, but when you consider that it has a root system that's been growing for almost ten years, it starts to look altogether more wonderful.

14. Feel Inspired by Bexell's Talking Stones

To say that Sweden has some of the quirkiest sights in Europe would be an understatement, and one of the most bizarre yet charming things that we have encountered in Europe is the talking stones of Bexell. Alfred Bexell was a landowner and Member of Parliament who lived in the 19th century. During this life, he engraved hundreds of stones in the forest of his property with sayings pertaining to history and philosophy. They were only discovered in 1925 by a family taking a picnic in the area.

15. Tuck Into a Bowl of Traditional Nettle Soup

You would think that anything that can sting you wouldn't taste very good. But think again, because nettle soup is one of the most traditional and beloved dishes to be found anywhere in Sweden. Believe it or not, nettle soup is a dish that dates back to 3000 years ago, and it's still popular with locals today, with a very green and healthy taste. It's also extremely cheap to make because nettle bushes abound around the country.

16. Wave a Rainbow Flag at Stockholm Pride

Sweden is one of the countries in the world that has a long history of being very progressive when it comes to LGBT rights, and we think that LGBT visitors should feel safe and have a great time in the country. And if you make it to Stockholm during the height of summer, you might have the chance to enjoy the annual festivities of Stockholm Pride, a Gay Pride event which draws over half a million spectators for its street parade every year.

(www.stockholmpride.org/en)

17. Walk Inside the Cavity of a Preserved Blue Whale

At up to 29.9 metres in length, the Blue Whale is the largest animal that has ever been known to exist. Of course, these whales live in deep ocean waters, and so it's very hard to get a sense of the scale of these magnificent creatures. That is unless you pay a visit to Gothenburg and the Malm Whale, the world's only mounted blue whale. It has its jaws hinged open, and you can step inside and lounge inside the whale's mouth with a cup of coffee.

18. Get a Caffeine Fix at Lisas Café & Hembageri

If you can't start your day before you have a hit of caffeine, fear not because Sweden is a nation of coffee lovers. In Stockholm, there are so many places to grab a decent cup of coffee and a pastry, but our favourite of them all is Lisas Café & Hembageri. We love it because of its local feel, its no-nonsense approach to food and drink, and because of the quality. Frothy milky drinks are strictly barred from the menu, so a straight up coffee and cinnamon bun it is.

(Skånegatan 68, 116 37 Stockholm)

19. Get to Grips With Norse Mythology at the Rok Runestone

Runestones play an important part in Old Norse culture, and they are essentially slabs of rock that are engraved with Runic inscriptions, telling stories of battles, kings, and more. One of the most important of these can be found in Sweden, and it's called the Rok Runestone. It actually contains the longest known Runic inscription, and is considered the first piece of Swedish literature. It dates all the way back to the 9th century, and you can see it up close beside the church in Rok.

(www.rokstenen.se)

20. Tuck Into a Shrimp Sandwich at Heaven 23, Gothenburg

Gothenburg, Sweden's second largest city, is often overlooked in favour of Sweden, but if you do have time to venture outside of the capital, we would highly recommend that you get to know this very charming place, and its wonderful food. When we're in Gothenburg, our favourite thing to eat is always the King Size shrimp sandwich at Heaven 23, which comprises 200 grams of delicious local shrimp in absolutely every sandwich. They sell 150,000 of these every year!

(Svenska Mässan, Mässans gata 22, 412 51 Göteborg; https://heaven23.se)

21. Take in a Twisted Skyscraper, Turning Torso

Sweden is not a part of the world that is very well known for having towering skyscrapers, and as you explore around the country you will find that many of the buildings are very low. Turning Torso, a skyscraper located in Malmo, is the exception to the rule, and it is actually the tallest building in all of Scandinavia. The

building has a neo-Futurist design, and gets its name because of the way it looks totally twisted and warped.
(Lilla Varvsgatan 14, 211 15 Malmö; www.turningtorso.se)

22. Check Out Ancient Rock Carvings in Tanum

If you are a history buff, there is plenty to explore in Sweden, and the rock carvings in the small town of Tanum are not to be passed over. The carvings here are some of the most complex and extensive Bronze Age carvings found anywhere in the world. Some of these designs date all the way back to 1800BC, and some of the things you will find depicted in the carvings are human figures, animals, and weapons, giving a fascinating insight into the lives and art of humans thousands of years ago.
(www.raa.se/upplev-kulturarvet/varldsarv/hallristningsomradet-tanum)

23. Take in the Winer Lights of Linkoping

While it's true that Sweden can be spectacularly dark and cold during the winter months, this is not to say that the country is totally devoid of charm at this time of year. In fact, the little city of Linkoping is at its most beautiful during the darkest months of winter, and this is because the city is lit up with thousands and thousands of neon lights and elaborate light installations. Some of the light installations have included chandeliers hanging from trees, disco balls hanging from bridges, and lots more.

24. Climb Aboard the World's Biggest Floating Museum

Sweden is a country with a proud maritime history, and if you'd like to learn more about this aspect of the country, you should definitely pay a visit to Maritiman in Gothenburg, the world's largest floating museum. Enter through the doors and you can explore the military ships of Sweden by actually climbing aboard. You can go below deck of a Naval submarine, see what life is really like on board a Destroyer ship, and much more.

(Packhusplatsen 12, 411 13 Göteborg; www.maritiman.se/en)

25. Explore the Sculptures of Millesgarden

The really charming thing about Stockholm is that it's a city comprising different island archipelagos, and each island has a very different feel. Some of the islands have many museums and restaurants that appeal to the tourist crowd, but we enjoy exploring some of the islands with less hype, like Lidingo. This island is very residential, but it doesn't mean that there's nothing to see. One of the loveliest things there is Millesgarden, a sculpture garden, which was the former residence and studio of sculptor Carl Miles.

(Herserudsvägen 32, 181 34 Lidingö; www.millesgarden.se)

26. Watch a Game of Bandy, a Local Winter Sport

If you are the sporty type, you might be interested in learning about one of the local sports in Sweden called Bandy. Bandy is actually one of the most loved winter sports in Sweden, but it's hardly even known outside of the country. It's basically a form of local ice hockey that dates all the way back to the Middle Ages. It's particularly popular in the north of the country when the lakes freeze over and provide perfect Bandy grounds in the open-air.

27. Explore Swedish Art at the Annual MARKET Fair

The Scandinavian countries are well known for their commitment to slick design, and you can get a sense of how creative the Scandi countries are on a visit to Stockholm's annual MARKET fair, which is hosted at the end of March each year. The works of artists from Sweden, Norway, Denmark, and Finland are showcased at the three day art fair where you can shop for a striking art piece to take home with you.

(www.market-art.se)

28. Discover 800 Years of History at Borgholm Castle

It's true that Sweden isn't as famed for its ancient history like some other parts of Europe like Greece or the UK, but we think this is largely down to the fact that the northern countries are somewhat isolated from the rest of the country, and there's actually a tonne to explore if you're a history buff. One of the most fascinating places is Borgholm Castle, which is now a ruin of the fortress that once was, dating way back to the 12th century. The inner courtyard also hosts summer concerts so it's well worth keeping up to date with the castle's programme of events.

(www.borgholmsslott.se)

29. Eat Yummy Buns at Swedish Bakery, Fabrique

Yes, it's true that France probably does have the best reputation for baked yumminess in Europe, but this is not to say that the French have a monopoly on delicious pastries, and this will certainly come to light of you visit Fabrique, a bakery that you can find dotted around various locations in Sweden. There are many delicious bites to enjoy, but we are particularly enamoured by their blueberry buns and sourdough bread.
(www.fabrique.se)

30. Keep Kids Entertained at a Pipi Longstocking Theme Park

Travelling with kids is a double edged sword. On the one hand, it's a huge privilege to be able to provide your kids with the kinds of memories that they'll carry with them for years to come, and on the other hand, it's a massive challenge to keep kids entertained all the time. But one place we are sure that all kids will love is Junibacken, a theme park that is centred around the Pippi Longstocking character. Inside, you and your kids will go on a journey through a magical fairytale world.
(Galärvarvsvägen 8, 115 21 Stockholm; www.junibacken.se/en)

31. Take in a Show at the Royal Swedish Opera

When you think of places around the world that are famous for opera and ballet performances, it's unlikely that Sweden would be the first country that springs in your mind, but this is not to say that there are not any opera companies or places to catch a show in the country, and the ultimate destination for any opera lover in Sweden would, of course, be the Swedish Opera House. In fact, this has been the national destination for opera since way back in 1773.

(Gustav Adolfs torg 2, 103 22 Stockholm; www.operan.se)

32. Explore Coral Cave, Sweden's Longest Cave

Sweden is a country that's just brimming with hidden treasures, and indeed, it's only in recent years that some of the country's most majestic natural features are being discovered. Take the Coral Cave, for example. This cave was only discovered in 1985, and until now only six kilometres of the cave have been properly explored, but this still makes it the longest cave in Sweden. You can only enter with a guide, but it's well worth doing so to feel the cool underground temperatures, and see the fascinating stalactites.

33. Go Back in Time at the Skansen Open Air Museum

Sweden is a country with an incredible agricultural history. If you'd like to get to know this part of the country's culture without actually having to get your feet dirty, we think that a visit to the Skansen Open Air Museum in Stockholm will be the answer to your prayers. This is actually the world's first open air museum, dating way back to 1891. Walk around, and you'll get to know country life in Sweden from Medieval times onwards. All the staff play characters, and there are tonnes of farm animals romancing around, which makes this the perfect place for a family outing.

(Djurgårdsslätten 49-51, 115 21 Stockholm; www.skansen.se/en/kategori/english)

34. Enjoy All the Thrills of Grona Lund

Sweden is typically thought of as a pretty sedate place. You can ride around the streets on your bicycle, and drink

some great coffee, but what if it's thrills and spills that you are looking for? Well, then you take yourself to Grona Lund, a famous amusement park in Stockholm, which was founded all the way back in 1883. It has fewer rides than some other parks, but its seaside location can't be beaten. You can also catch music concerts there in the summer.
(Lilla Allmänna Gränd 9, 115 21 Stockholm; www.gronalund.com/en)

35. Find Stockholm's Coolest Boutiques in Mood Stockholm

Something that you are bound to notice as you stroll the streets of Stockholm is that the local people typically dress very well indeed. And if you would like to take some of that effortless Scandi style home with you, there is only one place to go: Mood Stockholm. Mood is a relatively new addition to the city; a galleria that places a strong focus on forward thinking fashion and design. It's here that you'll discover all the coolest new local designers.
(Regeringsgatan 48, 111 44 Stockholm; http://moodstockholm.se)

36. Enjoy the Beach of Stockholm's Langholmen Island

Until fairly recently, Langholmen was one of the islands of Stockholm that you wouldn't have wanted to visit. That's because up until 1974 this was a prison island where criminals from around the country were sent. These days, however, Langholmen is a veritable summer paradise, and its particularly well known for its charming beach. On a sunny day, it's a beautiful spot to splash around and catch some rays.

(http://langholmen.com/en)

37. Have a Poptastic Day at ABBA: The Museum

Scandinavia has a reputation for producing some of the finest pop music that's ever been made, and when you consider that ABBA is a Swedish group, it should hardly come as any kind of surprise whatsoever. Well, if you want to experience a day of pure musical fun, make sure that you visit ABBA: The Museum while you are in Stockholm. This museum has many interactive elements, including a tour of their recording studio and the Eurovision Song Contest, which they won in 1974.

(Djurgårdsvägen 68, 115 21 Stockholm; www.abbathemuseum.com)

38. Indulge With a Slice of Vasterbotten Cheese Pie

While you are in Sweden, you will soon realise that the local people certainly do like to chow down on a bit of cheese, but we think that Vasterbotten cheese pie is the King of all cheese dishes in the country. This is a very simple dish with few ingredients, but it packs a hell of a punch. Basically, it involves Vasterbottensost cheese, which is a hard sharp cheese, being baked into a creamy custard filling. It's often enjoyed at summer picnics with crayfish.

39. Take a Ride on the Oresund Bridge

If you have some time to spare in Sweden and you feel like you can fit a trip to another country into your itinerary, this is actually very easily done as you can simply zip across the magnificent Oresund Bridge and find yourself in Denmark in minutes. The Oresund Bridge is the largest combined road and rail bridge in the world, and whether you decide to rent a car or take the train across, we're sure that it's a journey you won't forget.
(www.oresundsbron.com/sv)

40. Take to a Local Park for a Midsummer Celebration

Like other northern countries, Sweden is a country that is very much tied to the seasons, and this means that the height of summer, or Midsummer as it is known, is a cause for epic celebration. Midsummer always lands between June 20th and June 26th, and it's a wonderfully festive time to be in the country. To celebrate, people head out into the countryside, decorate maypoles with wreaths of flowers, and eat and drink into the night.

41. Party Under a Bridge in Stockholm

If you love nothing more than to party into the early hours of the morning, we can guarantee that you'll have a hell of a time in Stockholm, which abounds with fun bars and clubs. One of the most unique places where we have partied the night away is at Tradgarden, a club that is literally located underneath a bridge. In the summer months, the party is totally open air, and in the winter time it is sheltered so that you can party in comfort.

(Hammarby Slussväg 2, 118 60 Stockholm; www.tradgarden.com)

42. Embrace Your Inner Hippie at the Peace & Love Festival

Scandinavians have a reputation of being too cool for school, so a hippie-tinged festival might seem at odds with the local culture. But if you have a hippie living inside you that's just dying to burst out, you need to know about the annual Peace & Love Festival, which was actually Sweden's largest music festival for a long time. The festival is hosted in and around Borlange, and acts that have performed include the Sex Pistols, Keane, and Crystal Castles.

(www.peaceandlove.se)

43. Take In Some High Culture During the Gothenburg Culture Festival

Gothenburg may be an overlooked city in Europe, but honestly, it's the place to be if you are a culture lover. The Gothenburg Culture Festival is hosted every August, most of the performances and activities are free to attend, and over 1.5 million people take advantage of this opportunity each year. Whether you want to see an opera in the open

air, learn a circus skill, or watch a locally made film, there will be something for you to enjoy.
(http://goteborgskulturkalas.se/in-english)

44. Stay in an Underwater Hotel, the Utter Inn

Sweden offers a plethora of alternative accommodation choices, and certainly one of the most unique of the bunch is the Utter Inn, which looks like a floating house on the water, but hidden beneath you can actually find an underwater room where guests are welcome to stay. Once you make it to the middle of the island and this hotel, there is no way back without assistance, and so this is the perfect place to take in the air, and simply relax.
(Lake Mälaren, 722 12 Västerås)

45. Eat Traditional Swedish Fare at Prinsen in Sweden

When you are in Stockholm, there are so many restaurants to choose from that it can be hard to make any decision at all. But when we want a classic taste of Sweden in a cosy environment, we always return to Prinsen with its wood panelling and chandeliers. But, of course, it's the food that always steals the show. We recommend the herring platter in the summer, and the beef with fried potatoes and egg in the winter.

(Mäster Samuelsgatan 4, 111 44 Stockholm; http://restaurangprinsen.eu/en)

46. Head Back in Time During Visby's Medieval Week

If you get bored by walking from museum to museum but you would still like to learn about Sweden's history, we think that Medieval Week in Visby provides the most incredible opportunity to learn and have a whole lot of fun at the same time. In the second week of August, this town in Gotland provides the backdrop for a re-enactment of the Danish conquest in the mid 14th century. There's also a grand street procession, music playing in the streets, and lots of Medieval food to eat.

(www.medeltidsveckan.se/en)

47. Get Close to the Animals in Kolmarden Wildlife Park

If you are travelling with kids and want to give them some fun days out while you're away, a trip to the zoo is always a good idea, and where better than Kolmarden Wildlife Park, which is actually the largest zoo in all of Scandinavia? What's more, it's nestled in the countryside of Stockholm so you barely have to leave the city to have a taste of nature and get up close to beautiful moose, bears, giraffes, and lions.

(www.kolmarden.com)

48. Take in 20th Century Art at Moderna Museet

If you are an arts lover, Sweden might not be one of the first travel destinations that you think about visiting, especially when there are so famous arts cities like Paris, Florence, and London dotted around Europe. But this is certainly not to say that there is no arts culture to be found around Sweden, and one of our very spots for an artsy morning is Moderna Museet in Stockholm. The museum's collection contains works by the likes of Henri Matisse, Salvador Dali, and Pablo Picasso.

(Exercisplan 4, 111 49 Stockholm; www.modernamuseet.se/stockholm)

49. Try Fishing on Lake Storsjon

If your idea of the perfect holiday involves the quietude of sitting at the edge of a lake with a fishing rod in your hand, you'll be pleased to know that there are many places around Sweden where you can enjoy a spot of peaceful fishing. For our money, Lake Storsjon might just be the best of those places. The lake is located in a very remote part of the country, and it abounds with fish such as trout, char, grayling, whitefish, perch, roach, and more besides.

50. Kayak Around the Stockholm Archipelagos

Stockholm is a city with buckets and buckets of charm, and what makes it so special is that it's a city built on water with lots of little islands. Of course, one of the most fun ways to get to know this city is on the water itself. It's possible to take a boat tour, but if you feel like a more exciting adventure, it's also a great idea to go on a kayak tour around the archipelagos. Whether you want to paddle around for an afternoon or 3 days, there's a tour for you.

51. Indulge a Cinephile at the Stockholm International Film Festival

If you are a lover of great films, you will know how greatly Sweden has contributed to the international film scene, particularly those films created by Ingmar Bergman. Today, the country is still dedicated to producing great cinema, and you can get to grips with its cinema culture at the annual Stockholm Film Festival, which takes place every November. There are over 190 film premieres from more than 70 countries each year.
(www.stockholmfilmfestival.se/en)

52. Taste Hand Crafted Wine From Gotland

Europe is well known as a place that cultivates some of the most incredible wine in the world, but Sweden is not a country in Europe that most people would consider to be wine producing. But look hard enough, and you can even find this in Sweden. Gute Vineyard is a place in Gotland that produces around 6000 litres of wine each year, and visitors are welcome to check out the space and have a tasting.
(http://gutevin.se)

53. Enjoy a Lazy Beach Day at Ribersborgsstranden

When you think of beach destinations in Europe, it's very unlikely that the chilly waters of Sweden would be the first to appeal to you, but if you find yourself in Sweden at the height of summer, there are indeed some very charming beach locations that you can enjoy. One of our favourites, and a favourite among locals too, is Ribersborgsstranden in Malmo. Okay, the beach isn't natural and was created in the 1920s to give the local population a beach spot, but that doesn't make it any less charming.

54. Indulge in Pepparkakor Biscuits at Christmas Time

Although the winters of Sweden are cold and dark, the Christmas period is a whole lot of fun, and feels incredibly warm and festive in spite of the biting cold. We especially love all of the delicious Christmas food that appears on local tables during this period, designed to warm people with their comfort, and to be that little bit more indulgent. A Christmas favourite is always Pepparkakor biscuits, which are thin biscuits that are heavily spiced with pepper and ginger.

55. Feel the Grandeur of Uppsala Castle

Uppsala is a part of Sweden with huge amounts of charm. Forget the trendy boutiques and cafes of Stockholm and open up to a world of grand cathedrals and castles, and most notably Uppsala Castle. This castle was built in the 16th century, when Sweden was on its way to becoming a great European power, and played a huge role in the country's history. It's totally possible to spend a whole day touring the impressive grounds, and you can also find Uppsala Art Museum on the premises.

(Slottet, 752 37 Uppsala; www.destinationuppsala.se/sv/Gora/Gora/?tlang=sv&tid=721784)

56. Find Some Inner Peace at Yangtorp Sanctuary

One of the lovely things about taking a vacation is the practice of allowing yourself to relax away from the stresses of everyday life and really find some peace. Sweden is a place that can be great for providing this because there is so much beauty in the open space of the local nature, but also because of places likes Yangtorp

Sanctuary, a Chinese meditation centre, a place that you can visit for some healthy Vegan food and a meditation session.

(Jönstorp 8123, 242 96 Hörby; http://yangtorp.com/en)

57. Enjoy a Decadent Brunch of Toast Skagen

They say that breakfast is the most important meal of the day, and this is especially true when you are travelling and need as much energy as possible for days of sightseeing and activities. When we're in Sweden, our breakfast of choice is always Toast Skagen, which is an elevated way of eating toast for breakfast. It always includes shrimp with some other ingredients – perhaps some Dijon mustard, whitefish roe, and dill. Breakfast will never be the same again.

58. Visit a Stunning Baroque Structure, Skokloster Castle

When you think of magnificent Baroque architecture, you might not first expect to find it in Sweden, but actually Skokloster Castle is one of the best examples of grand Baroque architecture anywhere in Europe. Built in the mid

17th century by a great military commander, it is a product of the Swedish Age of Greatness when the country had huge control over the Baltic region. The interiors are just as grand as the exterior with gorgeous paintings, furniture, textiles, and more.

(http://skoklostersslott.se/sv)

59. Indulge a Sweet Tooth at Malmo Chokladfabrik

There are two kinds of people in this world: those who would drop everything for a chocolate fix, and those who we have no desire to know. And if you are one of the sensible people of the world who just can't get enough chocolate, Malmo Chokladfabrik is the place to be. This is a chocolate factory that dates all the way back to 1888 so they really do know about chocolate. They offer guided tours and tastings, and there is a shop on-site selling all of their yummy produce.

(Möllevångsgatan 36B, 214 20 Malmö; www.malmochokladfabrik.se)

60. Learn Something New at the Swedish History Museum

While it's true that Sweden can't quite boast about its selection of museums in comparison to other European cities like London and Paris, there's still enough in Stockholm for a few days of museum hopping, and one of the stand-out museums in the city is the Swedish History Museum. This museum covers the country's history from the Mesolithic period onwards, and is comprehensive to say the least. Our favourite part is The Gold Room, which contains over 3000 items made from 52kgs of gold.
(Narvavägen 13-17, 114 84 Stockholm; http://historiska.se/home)

61. Have a Chillingly Beautiful Night at Icehotel

Where are you expecting to stay in Sweden? Probably in a collection of hotels, guesthouses, and hostels, right? There's nothing wrong with that, but before you make your booking, we think that it's important that you know about Icehotel in a small northern village called Jukkasjarvi. This hotel and everything inside it is totally carved out of ice: the walls, the beds, the furniture, the bar, and everything else. No two rooms look the same, and staying here would be unforgettable.
(Marknadsvägen 63, 981 91 Jukkasjärvi; www.icehotel.com)

62. Visit an Iron Age Fort, Eketorp

If you're a history buff, make sure that you take the time to explore outside of Stockholm. This will allow you to see Swedish history beyond the museums and up close and in person. For example, Eketorp is an Iron Age Fort that dates all the way back to 400AD and you can still see it today. Since it was originally constructed it has been added to throughout the years and has served many purposes, such as a ringfort and a garrison. Guided tours are available throughout the summer.

(Eketorp borg, 380 65 Degerhamn; www.eketorp.se)

63. Stroll the Lavish Gardens of Solliden Palace

Solliden is one of the grandest and most beautiful places to visit in all of Sweden, and it's with good reason: this is a palace owned by the Swedish royal family, and it is still used as their summer residence during the summer months. It is also open to the public from May to September, and provides a great insight into the lives of the privileged. The gardens are particularly gorgeous, and perfect for a summertime stroll.

(http://sollidensslott.se)

64. Dance Your Socks Off at the Annual Bravalla Festival

When it comes to summer festivals, you might think that Glastonbury or Coachella is the way to go, but we think that Sweden's Bravalla Festival can give them a run for their money. This festival is only a few years old, but its already the biggest music festival in the whole country. Held in eastern Sweden at the end of June each year, it has attracted headliner talent such as Green Day, Rammstein, and Kanye West.

(www.bravallafestival.se/en)

65. Tuck Into the Saffron Pancakes of Gotland

Gotland is Sweden's largest island, and because it is separate from the mainland it has developed its own culture in many ways, including many gastronomic treats. Something that you can find only on this island is saffron pancakes, which are every bit as good as they sound. But they are not quite what you would expect, as this "pancake" is actually a type of saffron infused rice pudding that is baked in the oven with almonds, and then served with berries and cream.

66. Walk Through the Rainforest at Universeum

Sweden has lots of wonderful nature and incredible landscapes to explore, but it cannot claim to host anything as exotic as the rainforest. Or can it? Universeum is a huge seven floor science centre in Gothenburg that has constructed its own rainforest, so if you feel the need to escape to the Amazon, this could be just the ticket. You can walk through the rainforest on suspension bridges and get to know animals like monkeys and sloths.
(Södra Vägen 50, 400 20 Göteborg; www.universeum.se/en)

67. Party at a Music Festival in a Limestone Quarry, Into the Valley

Into the Valley is a fairly recent addition to Sweden's summer festival scene, but it's already gained a reputation as one of the most unique and special festivals in the country. This is because this festival is held each July in Dalhalla, an amphitheatre in the middle of nowhere that's constructed into a dug-out limestone quarry. The festival is dedicated to awesome electronic music, and stunning visuals combined with great music.

68. Indulge a Fashionista at Rohsska Museum of Fashion

You would think that Sweden's capital city, Stockholm, would be the centre of everything fashion related in Sweden, and while it is a fashionable place, we think that fashion lovers will have the most fun in Gothenburg, where the Rohsska Museum of Fashion is located. This museum contains over 50,000 gorgeous items from all over the world. There are haute couture garments from the runways of Paris, sumptuous textiles from Japan, and lots more to explore.

(Vasagatan 39, 411 37 Göteborg; http://rohsska.se/en)

69. Enjoy all the Thrills of Liseburg Amusement Park

Yes, there are lots of cafes and restaurants and museums and ancient sites to visit around Sweden, but what about the times when you really want to let loose and have some good old fashioned fun? That's when you find your way to Liseburg Amusement Park, which dates all the way back to

1923 and has even been chosen as one of Forbes' top ten amusement parks in the world. Highlights include a wooden roller coaster that reaches speeds of 90 km/hour and a creepy horror maze.
(Örgrytevägen 5, 402 22 Göteborg;
http://liseberg.com/en/home/Amusement-Park)

70. Go Back in Time and Visit a Viking Village

Something that the Swedes are famous for are their Vikings from centuries past. And we reckon that the most fun way to learn about this part of Swedish history is with a trip to Foteviken Viking Reserve, and open air museum that's more fun than any other museum you've visited. What's really special is that the people who live there actually live as the Vikings did around the clock, with ancient trades, and eschewing all modern technologies. Visiting is truly like stepping back in time.
(Museivägen 27, 236 91 Höllviken;
www.fotevikensmuseum.se/d/en)

71. Go Ice Fishing in Swedish Lapland

If you're that person who loves nothing more than to relax with a spot of fishing on the weekend, Sweden gives you the opportunity to take your fishing to the next level by ice fishing in the far reaches of Swedish Lapland. This is a completely different fishing experience altogether, and you will be guided out into remote parts of iced over water with snow shoes, you will dig into the ice, and then fish for Arctic fish native to the area.

72. Listen to Jazz at Fasching in Stockholm

When you find yourself in Stockholm on a Friday night, and you aren't sure how to entertain yourself, one of our favourite places to go to is Fasching, an institution of Sweden's jazz scene. This is a renowned Stockholm jazz bar than has been entertaining local punters since the 1970s. It's a great place to listen to some smooth sounds in the early evening, and if you want to extend the party it has weekend club nights that go on until 4am.

(Kungsgatan 63, 111 22 Stockholm; www.fasching.se)

73. Try Out Mushroom Picking in Vasteras

One of the lovely things about Sweden is that although you can find all different kinds of food, the cooks are always very committed to using seasonal, local produce to give a unique taste of Sweden, and something that abounds in the country are mushrooms. There are quite a few places where you can pick mushrooms, but of course you do need a guide and the central city of Vasteras is one place that provides them so you can learn about different types of mushrooms and have fun identifying them in the wild.

74. Stroll the Botanical Gardens of Visby

The medieval town of Visby has one of the most agreeable temperatures anywhere in Sweden, and this makes its botanical gardens, simply known as Botan, a wonderful place for strolling and enjoying some plant life that you won't see in other places in the country. Some of the plants and trees unusual to Sweden that you will find here include the tulip tree, handkerchief tree, empress tree, and vast blossoms of beautiful magnolia.

(Strandgatan, 621 55 Gotland; www.visbybotan.se/en)

75. Eat Swedish Pancakes With Whipped Cream and Berries

One of the best ways to start a day in Sweden is with a plate of heaped Swedish pancakes. How do these pancakes differ from other pancakes around the world? Well, they are actually quite a lot like French crepes, but more liquid is added to the batter in order to create an especially light texture. And beyond that, it's what the pancakes are served with that makes the difference. In Sweden, that means local berries and lashings of thick cream.

76. Indulge a Bibliophile at Stockholm Public Library

One of our favourite buildings in all of Stockholm has to be the Stockholm Public Library, which has been providing books to the local Swedish public since the 1920s. The most impressive part of the building is the central chamber, which as a cylindrical shape, and the circular walls of the room are absolutely heaving with books, more than 2 million of them actually.

(Sveavägen 73, 113 50 Stockholm; https://biblioteket.stockholm.se/bibliotek/stadsbiblioteket)

77. Listen to the Sounds of the Royal Stockholm Philharmonic

If classical music is what does it for you, then you absolutely need to know about the Royal Stockholm Philharmonic Orchestra who have a history that extends beyond 100 years and makes them the leading orchestra in the country. They play each year at the annual Nobel prize events, and also host two festivals a year at their home, the Stockholm Concert Hall.

78. Go Boating on Lake Malaren

Stockholm is a city with a huge amount of diversity, and on the outskirts of the city, you can even find a magnificent lake, Lake Malaren, where you can take fun boating trips to some of the parts of the city that are difficult to access by land, such as the Viking town of Birka. But truthfully you don't even need to have a destination, because it is so charming to take a trip on the water and feel the peace of the city's waters.

79. Find Some Cool Clothes at Bruno Vintage Market

The people of Stockholm have a certain effortless cool about them, and if you would like to take home a bit of the Stockholm style, the Bruno Vintage Market is a place where you can find one of a kind items at very affordable prices indeed. The area is also packed with cafes, so you can relax with a coffee and a cinnamon bun once you are done with your shopping adventure.

80. Dance Til You Drop at Summerburst

If you can't get enough of summer electronic festivals, you might not immediately think of Sweden as a place that caters to your party-hard needs, but think again, because you are invited to dance until you drop at Summerburst, an annual electronic festival, hosted in Stockholm each June. As well as attracting huge names like Deadmau5 and Steve Aoki, this festival is well known for its stunning light shows and pyrotechnics. There's also a twin festival in Gothenburg.

(www.summerburst.se)

81. Play Some Beach Volleyball at Tantolunden

Stockholm is not the kind of city where you are likely to feel overwhelmed by honking horns and oppressive city life. For a start, so many people cycle, and secondly, there are tonnes of green spaces that make it feel like you're in the country when you're in the city. A popular green space on the city island of Sodermalm is Tantolunden. There's tonnes of attractions here, including a beach volleyball court, mini golf, a frisbee golf course, and even sledding in the winter.

(Zinkens Väg, 118 67 Stockholm)

82. Get to Grips With Scandi-Design at the Nationalmuseum Design

Sweden is probably better known for its commitment to sleek design than to fine arts, and you can learn more about Scandinavian design at the Nationalmuseum Design, a new wing of the national art museum. Trendsters will be in their element on a visit here, with items showcasing the best of forward thinking fashion, slick furniture design, industrial design, ceramic arts and more from Sweden and the rest of the Scandi countries.

(Kulturhuset, Sergels Torg, 111 57 Stockholm; www.nationalmuseum.se/sv/English-startpage/About-us/Nationalmuseum-Design)

83. Surround Yourself With Butterflies in Stockholm

Stockholm is probably the last place on earth where you would expect to be surrounded by swarms of tropical butterflies, but that is exactly what you can experience if you visit the Butterfly House Haga Ocean in the city. You and your kids can wander freely inside the tropical greenhouse that contains many species of tropical butterflies. And there's also one of the largest shark tanks in Scandinavia.

(Haga trädgård, Hagaparken, 169 70 Solna; http://fjarilshuset.se)

84. Hit a Few Golf Balls at Barseback Resort

Yes, when you visit a new country it's wonderful to learn about the history and see the local attractions, but what if all you really want to do is hit a few golf balls? Well, with so much open space, Sweden can offer that too. In fact, there's just under 500 golf courses spread around the

country. With so much choice at your fingertips, we'd love to recommend Barseback Resorts. It has two championship courses, and mixes green, water, and beach.
(KLUBBHUSVÄGEN 5, 246 55 Skåne; www.barsebackresort.se)

85. Learn All About the Nobel Prize

One of the lasting legacies that has sprung from Swedish academia is the Nobel Prize. These days, everybody has heard of the Nobel Prizes for Peace, Literature, Science, and more, but did you know that these accolades started as the idea of a Swedish inventor, Alfred Nobel? Well, you can learn more about him and the prizes at the Nobel Museum in Stockholm.

(Stortorget 2, 103 16 Stockholm; www.nobelmuseum.se)

86. Eat at a Two Michelin Star Restaurant, Faviken Magasinet

It's no secret that Sweden is one of the more expensive countries to visit in Europe, and while you may not be able to afford to eat at high-end restaurants for your entire trip, we think that it's a good idea to have at least one fine

dining experience, and there is nowhere finer than Faviken Magasine, which is located in the middle of nowhere, but it's worth finding. You can expect nothing short of extreme decadence, and the 20 course tasting menu is certainly a dining experience you'll never forget.
(FÄVIKEN 216, 830 05 Järpen; http://favikenmagasinet.se/en)

87. Visit the Jokkmokk Winter Market

One of the best ways to learn about the local culture in a country is to visit a local market, and get the feel for local trade, food, and traditional items. For our money, the most charming of all the markets in Sweden is the Jokkmokk Winter Market in Swedish Lapland. This is more than just another trendy farmers' market, because it has a 400 year history, and was started by indigenous people in the north. It's only held across one weekend in February, and it's the ultimate place to buy authentic handicrafts made by indigenous communities.
(www.jokkmokksmarknad.se/visitors)

88. Have a Wreck Diving Adventure off the Coast

If you are a keen diver, Sweden will almost certainly not be the first country that appeals to you for a diving an adventure. And yes, there are no tropical fish, and there are no coral reefs. But what you can find off the coast of Sweden is something just as magical and fascinating – hundreds and hundreds of wrecked ships. One of the best wreck dives is around the Stockholm Archipelago, where you'll find Riksnyckeln, a Swedish battleship lost all the way back in 1628.

89. Relax in a Basement Bath House

Although Stockholm is a very fun city where there is lots to see and do, there might be times when you just want to relax and unwind. It's in those moments that we head to Storkyrkobadet, one of the least known but most interesting spots in the entire city. This 17th century building was originally a Dominican convent, and was later converted to a school where the vaults contained baths for the children. Later on a sauna was built, and it's a charming if simple bathhouse in the heart of the city today.

(Svartmangatan 20, 111 29 Stockholm; http://storkyrkobadet.se)

90. Drink Magnificent Swedish Beer at Omnipollo's Hatt

Europe has an incredible beer culture, and microbreweries creating their own delicious beers are popping up in the most unexpected of places. Our favourite spot for a delicious local beer in Stockholm has to be Omnipollo's Hatt. There's a great selection of ten local beers on tap, and they also make pizzas in-house, and if pizza and beer isn't a combination made in heaven, we don't know what is.

(Hökens gata 1A, 116 46 Stockholm; www.omnipolloshatt.com)

91. Sleep in the Forest at the STF Kolarbyn Eco-Lodge

Sweden is the perfect place if you want to leave the pressures of city life behind you and get back to nature, and we can think of no better place to immerse ourselves in nature than at the STF Kolarbyn Eco-Lodges. These huts in the wood are located just two hours out of Stockholm, but are a world away in every other respect. Here there is no electricity, no showers, wooden beds without mattresses, and the joy of being right there in the forest where you can swim in the lake and see wild moose, beavers, and more.

(Skärsjön, 739 92 Skinnskatteberg; http://kolarbyn.se/en)

92. Enjoy the 6km Beach of Angelholm

If you are like many other people and love nothing more than to relax with some beach time while you're on holiday, Sweden might not be your first choice of holiday destination. But look hard enough, and you can actually find some very charming beaches around the country. And one of the least developed and most charming spots in Angelholm. There is a whopping 6 kilometres of beach to be enjoyed here, and also many small galleries and ceramics studios to explore when you aren't lying on the sand.

93. Climb to Sweden's Highest Peak, Kebnekaise

Are you the adventurous sort? You'd rather strap on your hiking boots than stroll around the aisles of museum? Then you might want to get familiar with Kebnekaise, Sweden's tallest mountain, which has a height of 2097 metres above sea level. Fortunately, there are several routes to the peak, so whether you have lots of climbing experience or not, there are definitely ways you can do it. If you do take a more challenging route, be sure to hire a guide who knows the terrain.

94. Eat a Traditional Swedish Sausage, Isterband

If you happen to be visiting Sweden in the autumn or winter months, you'll need to fill yourself with food that can warm you from the inside out, and one of our favourite local comfort foods is called Isterband, a type of local sausage. This smoked sausage is made from pork, barley groats, and potato. When served with creamed dill potatoes and sauerkraut, you have the unique taste of Sweden on a plate.

95. Be a Knight for the Day at the Royal Armoury

The Royal Museum in Stockholm is more than just another museum. For a start, it's the oldest museum in the whole country and dates right back to 1628, and secondly you can actually find it within the stunning Royal Palace. This is the place to learn all about Swedish military history and royalty, and it makes learning about these things a really fun experience. You can even get your kids to try on dresses and knight costumes.

(Slottsbacken 3, 111 30 Stockholm;
http://livrustkammaren.se/en)

96. Feel the Power of Hallingsafallet Waterfall

What is more stunning than a gushing waterfall? It's a beautiful sight to be behold and it can make you feel totally connected to nature and the world around you. There's quite a few waterfalls to explore in Sweden, and we think that the most magnificent of the bunch is the Hallingsafallet Waterfall, which is located pretty much in the middle of nowhere in Jamtland County. But it is worth seeking out. Its drop is over 43 metres into a beautiful canyon.

(830 90 Strömsund Municipality)

97. Take a Boat Trip to Birka, Sweden's Viking City

If you are interested in the local history of Sweden, you will no doubt want to learn more about the Vikings, their lives in Sweden, and how they influenced the country, and so what better way to explore than to visit Birka, an actual

Viking city? It is situated on an island called Bjorko in the middle of a lake on the edge of Stockholm, and contains a reconstructed Viking village, weaved cabins, archaeological fields, and lots more fun stuff.

(Björkö, 178 92 Ekerö; www.birkavikingastaden.se/en)

98. Walk the Quaint Streets of Sigtuna

Sweden has a lot of charm in its own right, but if you would like to explore a little way outside of the city, you'll have a charm overload in the little town of Sigtuna, which lies just north of the capital. While there are no epic museums, it's a lovely place to amble around and pass a pleasant sunny day. In fact, it was Sweden's first town, created in the 10th century. There are lots of charming wooden houses, cafes, and the local people are very friendly.

(http://destinationsigtuna.se/en)

99. Visit the Mackmyra Distillery to Try Swedish Whisky

While Ireland and Scotland might be more famous for its whisky production that Sweden, there is certainly a whisky

culture there, and actually, what better way could there be of warming up in the Swedish cold than by taking a wee nip of the good stuff? If you do happen to be a whisky lover, the Mackmyra Distillery is the ultimate place to get a schooling in Swedish whisky production. There's also a restaurant on-site with great local food.
(http://mackmyra.com/besok/whiskybyn)

100. Celebrate Winter at the Kiruna Snow Festival

If you can brave the cold, Sweden becomes an altogether different place in the wintertime, and we think that you can experience all the charm of a Swedish winter at the Kiruna Snow Festival. The festival takes place each year at the end of January, and it's an epic celebration of everything wintry, icy, and snowy. You will find cross country skiing, outdoor theatre in the snow, snow sculpting competitions, and loads more fun besides.
(www.snofestivalen.com/english)

101. Eat Sweden's Best Ice Cream at 18 Smaker

We can't pretend that Stockholm always has warm and sunny weather, but when the sun is shining down on the

Swedish capital, there is nothing we enjoy more than ambling along the waterside with an ice cream in hand, and it's a known fact in Stockholm that the most delicious local ice cream is served at 18 Smaker. They use organic ingredients, and the local flavours are incredible. Think black liquorice, cardamom, or lingonberry.

(Hornsgatan 64, 118 21 Stockholm; www.18smaker.se)

Before You Go...

Thanks for reading **101 Amazing Things to Do in Sweden.** We hope that it makes your trip a memorable one!

Have a great trip!
Team 101 Amazing Things

Made in United States
North Haven, CT
13 December 2022